SELECTED POEMS 1970-1980

WITHDRAWN

Donated to
SAINT PAUL PUBLIC LIBRARY

Andrei Codrescu

Selected Poems
1970-1980

NEW YORK 1983

ACKNOWLEDGEMENTS

These poems appeared in the following magazines: *The World, Lillabulero, Pro-Ject, Theo, Tractor, Toothpaste, Buffalo Stamps,* SUN, *Boulder, Big Sky, The Milk Quarterly, Isthmus, Alternative Press, Search for Tomorrow, Poetry, The Poetry Review* (London), *The Human Handkerchief, Ironwood, Gum, Manroot, Stuffed Crocodile, Bastard Angel, Doones, Defiance, Deserted Times, Fervent Valley, Amphora, The End, Features, Clear Creek, Streets & Roads, Out There, The Periodical Lunch, Blue Suede Shoes, Hearsay Broadsides, Unmuzzled Ox, The Chicago Review,* and *Beatitude.*

They also appeared in the following books, whose publishers are credited in the author bibliography: *License to Carry a Gun; The History of the Growth of Heaven* (1971); *the, here, what, where; A Serious Morning; The History of the Growth of Heaven* (1973); *grammar & money; Secret Training; For Max Jacob; The Marriage of Insult and Injury; The Lady Painter; For the Love of a Coat; Necrocorrida.*

Printed in the United States of America

First Edition

Library of Congress Cataloging in Publication Data

Codrescu, Andrei, 1946-
    Selected poems, 1970-1980.

    I. Title.
PS3553.03A6   1983   811'.54   82-19532
ISBN 0-915342-38-3

The publication of this book is supported by a grant from the National Endowment for the Arts in Washington, D.C., a federal agency.

For Alice

Contents

SELECTED POEMS 1970-1980

FROM

LICENSE TO CARRY A GUN
(1970)

THE LICENSE TO CARRY A GUN
BY JULIO HERNANDEZ

for John Sinclair

The License to Carry a Gun *was supposedly written in jail by a Puerto-Rican poet. Julio is a scout into a political future of prison reality, a sacrificial lamb. He taught me survival. He was born on the Lower East Side in 1967; he is hovering saintly on the edge of all my action; hernandez like miguel and julio like my father.* AC

FROM A TRILOGY OF BIRDS

in birds is our stolen being. from summer to summer
they carry on my destruction, more obvious
as i get closer to death.
in the kitchen powerful lights stay on at night
watching the summer passage of birds.
the sea contains
their thick excrement, our longing to fly,
the sea changes color.
weak ships over the water.
i am seasonal.
i offer poisoned lights to passing birds
through the guarded door of the kitchen.
it suddenly opens.
i catch the sea when it is taken away
by disciplined clouds of birds.

FIDEL CASTRO

he's got jesus dead by gun behind his motorcycle eyes,
he holds my soul on a theory bail,
rocking my country with a skinny peasant
he holds from the belt.
same peasant feeds birds at the border.
i counted so many languages in the dark
spoken by an old cuban refugee,
owner of a coca cola fountain of dead tactics,
south of havana.
my tongue is dead now,
its meat hangs like a belt
from the hand of fidel.
dubious birds
burn over the snow at the border.

THE LICENSE TO CARRY A GUN
to andrei codrescu

they will forever refuse you the license to carry a gun
but i am a gun and paolo and john and grazzia
(remember her forked tongue?)
the license to carry a gun is a license to be.
patricius, brutus, don quixote come naked
to my mind vs. target!
they're full of shit by daylight
but when lights go out in these cells
they are my loaded darkness,
my license to carry a gun.

RAIN

rain cuts an exit in the wall
for him who is of rain. a square hole
westward. through which the men of rain
will fly.
they prayed to water for a very long time,
they sold what they could.
the bald burglar from indiana
whose name should be silent.
silvio and his american friend, the dope pusher
from harlem, jack, one-eyed and singer
and all men who have children.
rain cuts an exit   wet like cunt
in lonely nights from very left

there is an orange rotting on the table
closer to freedom than i ever was.
i'll throw it away soon, its smell
gives me the same sweet hallucinations
i had when i was holding a gun.
orange of sun, my useless state of mind

ALL WARS ARE HOLY
BY PETER BOONE

All Wars Are Holy *was conceived as a book by an ex-beatnik who became a sort of mystical Fascist in Vietnam or somewhere else. Peter Boone is dead. He was accidentally killed when a bullet struck Garcia Lorca. They were linked by an umbilical cord 30 years long.* AC

WINTER IN ISTANBUL

Such is the loneliness here.
the birds over some town in new jersey
try to imitate airplanes
and fall dead in the snow.
can't think of anything that bad.
outside the window
a moving theatre.
images of my previous winters.
a play called
freedom.
it isn't death or loneliness.
it's my capacity to wonder
fading in the dawn of the bosphorus
along with my taste for strange politics.
i should invent a woman
to shoot me with her fresh body
of winter.
farewell, black emigrant fantasy,
you who wear sunglasses at night
defending your emigrant body.
our winters meet here.
you make the birds bearable.

WOMB AND CITY

i start my fridays like a fecundity
ritual.
i throw eggs at tourists
and lift their skirts and sunglasses.
fridays remind one of birth,
of the new baby crushing against
the white walls of the hospital.
his long belly full of magic.
the body of a red cat glued to the mind
of a dead witch-mother.
fridays are the womanly ways
of this bombed city.
the mosques are golden females
and i am dying for cunt.

BLUES ARE AMERICAN HAIKUS

the dead horse
holds a blue note in his yellow teeth.
the white people of turkey
pass by without looking.
minus that stare,
his death is almost complete.
it snows on a page of the
daily american
near the dead horse's mouth.
i might as well be snowed-in in a church
thinking of dead horses.
black skin brings spring.
oh how cold it is in america
since the death of its niggers.

howard johnson's is covered with snow,
dead horse hamburgers.
welcome to turkey,
black souls

ALL WARS ARE HOLY

what happened to me.
it isn't only this war in vietnam.
it's the war of my blood,
the small wars in immaculate labs,
the war of children in the flesh of assaba,
the wars in cosmos over the heads of philosophers.
death, magnetic void of my balance,
beloved one of my sanity,
your silk shoes are soft in the dreams of my brothers.
you finish the milk in the glass
of the rebellious husband
and give sleep to his pain-ridden mate.
don't touch me,
i am your holy mouth

GIST

america is healthy. i am healthy
in the body of christ.
the fall of melted metal builds
my spheric soul.
i go first.

my body's laid flat
on the copper table
and pounded up thin like a sheet
to pick up prophecy.
six holes are drilled in my body.
the marketing of this new instrument
is now in the hands of pan.
i am healthy. I wish
that i had one thousand such instruments.

DRUMS AND BELIEVERS

be true in women like a throat
made ethical by the knife.
i bleed in my drums to make her return.
the believers are tied to the drums in the night
or maybe their skin
is laid on the drums
to make her return.
i can wait like a saint
for the rhythm of my drums
to meet the rhythm of your heart
somewhere on the roads of america.
the holy beat of your body
slides white in the mind of the drums.

TESTING. TESTING.

whatever you say, paola francesca di virgine,
leader of mute nuns through the candles of my ideas,
whatever you desire.
see, we could turn the water pipes
into lances shields armors and crosses
and any useless offensive paraphernalia
you prefer.
half of my knighthood offers itself to you
in that sentence.
have some meat from my left arm
and all the fish from this paper bag
and my new refrigerator,
conserver of god.
and of milk.
i'll stare at your cross if you say so
till i decompose.
the landlord knocks at the door
and steps on my masked face full of moss
turned blue-eyed to the mad cross
of your impertinence.
well, he says.
there seems to be a question as to your existence.
i am happy to answer that
by punching myself in the mouth.

Poems From the River Aurelia
by Alice Henderson-Codrescu

Dedicated to all the women I have ever known
and in particular to:

> *my mother*
> *rosa luxemburg*
> *tristan tzara*
> *Rrose Sélavy*
> *valerie solanas*
> *sonya tolstoy*
> *daniele hibou*
> *alice henderson-codrescu*
> *myrna loy*
>   *and*
> *aurelia munteanu*

The woman in man is maybe the most unknown woman ever;
this fascinated and obsessed me for a few years. At one point in
California, the woman came back to me; this book is the begin-
ning of my search for this Lady in English. The feeling was of a
"notice of health" from the River Aurelia, a river which has never
been sick, polluted with melancholy.

The River Aurelia is fictitious, but it flows nevertheless: its name
comes from Aurelia M., my first wife. Four years ago in Rome, I
wrote a long epic poem in which I established a new mythology:
of moon worship, anti-civilization, permanent migration, perma-
nent revolution: the women go under the earth to build a female
world while outside, in the sun, men make themselves women of
salt. That myth reverberates several times in the book. That much
for genesis.   AC

13

REVERSE

a poem for rosa luxemburg who lost it all one summer
but next there it was,
on the other side of a gilded german window.

i, too. born on the other side, alongside
an intricate, painful brain,
in the deep snows of the barbarian kingdom,
a state of permanent sorrow.
the horses unmoved in the warm stables.
beat the ground you were born on,
lash it with your later female skins,
screw your breasts into it,
unveil, unearth.
a country of women.
at some depth we find each other, rosa,
i find your profile obsessing hamburg,
moscow and london.
i'm not nervous any longer,
nerves are short and the longest bone in my body
is black, the longest
year in your memory stops short
of witchcraft.
there is alcohol in your blouse,
revolution is alcohol left over,
the countryside is still fermenting it.
tastes like hell.
rosa luxemburg,
i'm cold and new york is a white city.
the warm glove of your assassin's hand
lies on my table,
dinner for a friend

ZZZZZZZZZZZZZ

i want to touch something sensational
like the mind of a shark. the white
electric bulbs of hunger moving
straight to the teeth.
and let there be rain that day over new york.
there is no other way
i can break away from bad news
and cheap merchandise.
(the black woman with a macy's shopping bag
just killed me
from across the street.)
it is comfortable to want
peace from the mind of a shark.

FOR MARG
SO SHE COULD FUCK AGAIN

i want to clean the lover of the dead warrior
take that strangeness out of her
like a poisonous herb
for my hands to remember.

if you lived through the livers of warriors
kneel near those ladies locked in their hearts,
cut the chain between their knees.
clean prayer, lord of thighs,
make your body go past
the black iron balls of the hero,
past the half-eaten subway in the fork of his memory.
the rats and the rain like an envelope.

i kneel and i clean you,
i put back the flame in your cunt
out of my own.
let's move to the rhythm of my body,
over the lordly gold of the dead in the rain

1st avenue basics

if you fight guerrilla warfare in a green skirt
down 1st avenue
leave your breasts at home.
that goes for running guns too.
perfumed high-class mouths blow pearled-handled pistols.
these are the basics of 1st avenue.
the beauty in the hand. basics for a new poetry.
then you warm to your heart
kleenex used by maria dolores.
this helps you erase every trace of your passage.

DREAM DOGS

years ago it was easy to dream of wolves
and wake up your lover
to show him the blood on your hip.
the wolves had ties
and followed after every sentence
rather polite.
now there are police dogs
using tear gas and the lover next to you
doesn't wake up.

DAWN

three times, yearly, my breasts dawn painlessly
into a cycle unknown,
i am struck.
a thing like dawn escapes the hand,
blinds the hypnotist,
throws the witch in wild confusion.
poetry, its opposite.
my lower body crawls with beggars
like a medieval city prospering in the ruin of its neighbors.
tea merchants getting fat.
my mind, restructured to resemble a gun,
a miraculous gun of known deeds, heroic
resemblances. the upper hand
of affinities.
i, like a merchant, fat,
i roll by on a thick carpet, touching,
untouching.
i love to scream in mornings like this,
to awaken a dawn ancestry

BEACH IN SEBASTOPOL, CALIFORNIA

whoever found this beach alone, maybe in 1723,
was beautiful: a young indian
who laid his girl in the sand, smoked some,
barked at the sea. the fishes, the firecrackers
of the sea going out at his feet.
damn all time, even his. even then
someone was dreaming already of building new york,

within horses
cars were stirring. now, i love him
whoever he was in 1723. i ride
his horse, he drives my volkswagen,
i am his,
he discovers my beach and we sit at the sea
and the breeze opens books.
the hooks of the occult jam the sewing machines.

POEM FOR KYRA

paradise too is a schizophrenic slum,
a holy octopus with rooms to let
and the four rooms on the left are taken,
it smells as if they are frying angels in there.
in here you smile,
cheat the barefoot goddess at dice,
she doesn't know any better
she's busy unbuttoning your shirt,
feeling your thigh.
you lean on her breasts,
you're maybe ready to die or maybe
it is only dice you're going to play.
for the sheep no danger.
unless you go farther
or take me with you.
then paradise: a thousand strong women
armed with flamethrowers and loaded pussy
storming the streets of the world

FROM

The History of the Growth of Heaven
of Heaven

(1971)

The History of the Growth of Heaven

As a funny monk one is never sure where
the wind blows the candelabras over the heads
of Fathers at work,
the light of Purgatory.
The funny monks are at the flanks of cheese
and wine, it helps redemption
to savour out the scales of the cell's
square gated window.
I suppose this in a way is a Revolutionary speech,
monks against Fathers or the monk inside Father's
account of the monk.
Good journey then to the illuminati
who set their heavy paws into the highway, drifting
to the wind, outside,
the fences grow the crazes of a giant ferry

To the Virgin as She Now Stands to the Monk after a Beatles Movie

This is no cell, Holy Woman,
this is a lookout into the shape of that boundless forgery,
into the outline of the Devil's face
when the smog opens up to let us view
the rugged cliffs of his face.
This, of course, is a Monk's crossview
of the book between the legs of naked ladies,
those splinters of you
who go to the movies by themselves
to make love in the dark.

For a flash the singer reaches out on the wire
of your Presence, through the screen,
it hurts to see the waste.
Paralysis of upper vastness, Virgin,
caste out, caste in
of my race.
The terror of your cunt is the beauty of your face.

FAITH RELEARNED

A letter to Father Veitch

Faith is the evidence of things I've wasted,
the evidence of things not seen
maybe the canals of Amsterdam could tell you
where I've been all these years:
partly behind my shoulder blades
scratching the skin's illusion of secret showers,
partly fighting an ancient war,
partly trying to fit a rug on this floor,
Woolworth's, $9.95, no good,
and partly monking in my cell:
the cheese they feed you here muffles your yell,
its holes let in the others',
its holes look out of you:
the things they've seen inside my night
draw blood from the hinges of lovers,
from the owls of Holland at night.
What I see through my cheese holes is
that view the crucifix has
from inside the iron shirt of the Knight
as he bops past crazy windmills

MY NEXT BOOK

My next book will have a poem for each
Saint dropped by the Church,
33 poems in all,
the longest one for Saint George
who was the longest man in the world when added
to the end of his lance.
I will put a little cross by each poem
meaning "here lies,"
a very deceptive move since no one
will lie in there,
no one, not even the Monk
who will be out thinking of girls
what are poems?

THE SIN OF WANTING A NEW REFRIGERATOR

Sin is impervious
to past transmutations
yet this is how it happened:
I desired
the bareness of my cell to open
in the vaster bareness of a new refrigerator,
it,
    the refrigerator,
having come all the way from the First Avenue of my
New York days,
from the fruit stand of the dark
fat merchant.   He opened it up
in another Universe: the milk bottles inside
lit up like Angels. First Avenue

refrigerated. I was a penny short
and I still am.
They tell me here that new refrigerators
are forbidden, oh
that penny had in it a sin
as elemental as the copper
it was made of

MORE ABOUT POEMS

I want to write down the life
that could be my life if I insisted
if I pulled up a corner of the cloth to let the lady
with the groceries
have a look at my cock,
flash of storks running errands for God.
I want to perfect a partial view
through a hole in my cloth,
a slanted recording, a window hangup,
not mindful of the undistorted door,
of the remarkable way.
I ought to repair my life with the grease of Poems:
the bourgeois at war with the monk.
Oh, the volume of the devil's lease!

The Status of the Monk

is not moveable
though your block might be getting worse
and the crickets are moving out. From porch to porch
the twisted ladies have
turned their knitting needles on themselves,
housewife collage.
A people's militia to meet the needs of love.
But I have nothing left to hate,
I remain medieval
no matter what you do to me,
perched on myself like an endless tapestry,
God put his suitcase down to rest on it.
The women try to guess its contents.

About Photography

I hate photographs,
those square paper Judases of the world,
the fakers of love's image of all things.
They show you parents where the frogs of doom
are standing under the heavenly flour,
they picture grassy slopes
where the bugs of accident whirr twisted
in the flaws of the world.
It is weird,
this violence of particulars
against the unity of being

ATTEMPT TO SPELL, INCANTATE AND ANNOY

May his eyes go on unblinking
and his ears from bells unhurting
may he go the way of wires . . .
I can't write spells, I'm a monk.
One is constantly expected to write about his environment,
the melting stuff, the mood of his sins,
the geology of the billionth of a second,
I am even supposed to confess my environment
to an asthma struck intermediary of a not-so-instantaneous God.
Do you, Holy Ones, suppose
that we are made of thick flesh, rawhide, penicillin,
or is the Confessor really Nylon Man
when he chooses to rip open his ecclesiastic cloth
and go chasing after bank robbers?
I had to put this heresy down on paper
this poem is a heretic environment
how do you confess it?

THE FIRST ICON WITH GUN

Flemish style, late 17th century:
the Virgin holds a gun
not the baby.
Artist, unknown.

More about Monks

Monks don't look at themselves in the mirror
in the rectory hallway, going to confession,
they don't even look into those symbolic mirrors
whose growth
we are encouraged to nurture.
The fact is Monks are blind.
Which reminds me of a dream:
Rembrandt was complaining about the destruction
of his best paintings
but he contended that they could still be seen
in an astral plane as astral paintings.
Which plane, I said,
but a screen slid silently and God the Father
grabbed Rembrandt by his hair

Stanley the Archer

When we become acquainted
he asks what did you do before you were a monk
and there is a light breeze from the ocean
this far inland.
He explains:
it must be the coming age breezing through the assholes of angels.
It is and I used to be
the Peyton Place dentist on TV

Junk Mail

Junk mail. A gun for a dollar.
This one dollar deal has changed the face
of all I thought was mine,
and it still cries from the enormous pain
of being screwed inside my shoes,
made to reside upright,
both eyes directed into the heart of "Daily News"
and snow will be here soon.
The stamp stares me down with "Man on the Moon."
I smell the blades of cold
travelling this side of mail without zip code,
glued to the wide phantoms of cars going out
of style. My snowed in prayers will relieve my heart
of bombs and rifles.
For awhile

Howdy

Before I was a monk I had a cat.
She was darker than Buddha, the great, the elementary.
Actually she was black
and she liked bad wine which she licked
from my glass when I went out
looking for girls.
Her drunk look was of drowned dogs,
of sorrowful junk,
she had seen my brother François
hung from his laces outside his lady's castle.
From the height of her whiskers it looked like the facts of heaven.

Now I'm a monk and Howdy,
'twas her name,
peeps backward into my mouth from a ceiling
of frosted eternity.
the bad wine links us like a birthday feeling

Souls Looking for Bodies

The pregnant women are jealously guarded by their Angels,
perched over them like moist blossoms,
fighting the Souls come to enter.
If the Angel sleeps
the Soul enters.
There is no real choice,
only the sudden loss of vigilance

The Ghouls of Candlemas

stick to the holly.
Where did you go from Christmas until now?
I went skiing with my slaves on the Virgin Snows
to prepare for love, for the New
World jutting forth from the sinews of New
Hampshire. In the old days
they had Inspectors throwing out the holly
from Church, for Candlemas.
Now the ghouls are going crazy with the candles
and our auras flicker

(for Alice)

The Holy Grail

When they bring in the Dish
the Cup disappears suddenly for many centuries
and before they get to eat
the King sends everyone looking for the Cup
by which time the Dish is gone.
Lately I've been monking at this.
Why does a grown man write poems?
What's an overgrown monk doing away from God
with a typewriter?
Maybe a grown man builds houses.
What does it really matter
what a grown man does
what a grown man is.
This time the Dish is missing.

Symmetry

Sooner or later
everyone finds out who his Murderer is
and most times it lies in bed next to him
holding him by the murder weapon.
For a monk it is harder to guess,
weapon and Murderer belong to another world:
there are no identities to point out
only reflections.
Sometimes a word blows up like a bomb.

FROM

THE, HERE, WHAT, WHERE

(1972)

CRIMES

when angels
commit crimes
these are
then
transferred
into
the heart
of god
where
they find
older
crimes
waiting
for something

GUILLOTINE

in france
they hold
the severed head
to the eyes
of the people.
what the
head says
is
never
recorded.
the
people
never
remember

EXECUTION

        when they
                shoot
    put
your mouth
                on your palm
        and
            suck
    your
        lifeline
out
of
it!
        this way
they will be shooting
                        nothing
            an egg
a brand new
man
        with a
                blank
        fate

ARTHUR BREMER BLUES

lyndon johnson is dead
de gaulle is dead.
franco is dead.
kosighin is dead.
and the new pope too.
nobody to shoot.

REVOLUTION

the key
to this
the key
to that.
what do you
need
keys for
if we are gonna
break down
all the
doors?

FROM

A SERIOUS MORNING

(1973)

JUNK DAWN, NYC

greeks mounted on needle points
drop through asia minor
into our veins via new york
and the room fills with the pure
products of my imagination like a rag
with gasoline. for no particular
reason the floor is sooty and the small
buddhas crouching in the corners
are sick with a fragrance
of hair. there is nowhere to go
save inside yourself: there everything
is slightly demented and free

POLITICS

you are in a barbed land and you are NOT dying.
the claws of the grass are bent
inwards. likewise the trees are tearing nothing
but their own hearts. everything holds in
the bleeding meat of self-injury.
surrounded by protection from each other
we have left the inside
vulnerable.
it is the walls i hate with all my heart
and those who, dead inside,
have built them from their own disfigured corpses

BOOKS

death covers me with fine dust.
i love used fat books. they are
like used fat bodies coming out of sleep
covered with fingerprints and shiny
snail trails.
i want to read the way i love:
jumping from mirror to mirror like a drop of oil
farther and farther from my death.
but god gives us fat books and fat bodies
to use for different reasons
and less a metaphor i cannot say
what is that haunts me

WORK

at night the day is constantly woken up
by exploding dream objects
until our days are tired
and collapse on our hearts like loud
zippers breaking in the middle.
i sleep in the daytime with my head on the piano.
i sleep at night too standing on the roof.
i sleep all the sleep that is given me plus
the sleep of those who can't sleep and the sleep
of great animals who lie wounded
and unable to sleep.
i'm dead tired from the work everyone does
ceaselessly around me, from the work the morning
crowds are going to do after they are thrown up
by the thousand mouths of toast and cologne
into the buses and subways,

from the work the plants do to get water
from the labors of beasts looking for meat
from the labors of speaking replying writing
from the work going on inside me with a million
greedy cells beating the shit out of each other
from the work of the sun turning around
and the earth turning around it.
i'm tired in general and sleepy in particular.
i have a great desire to move elsewhere.

SATURNIAN DILEMMA

i am a vision looking for a way out of
my head. i have a head in every window
of an endless row of houses. i have a hand
in every refrigerator. moon lit
french fries drive me to frenzy. i have
envisioned telling the truth which is what
my body consists of. every time
i have been stopped
by my appetite

TÊTE-À-TÊTE

my body, spill-proof but not quite,
is full of grinning groceries. my liver
dreams of pâté. my heart
makes the soup red. my head
stuffs itself with birds. even
my fingernails look good in jello.

the trick is to bring in each
dish at the right time in the dim
candlelight. the trick
is to surprise your guest with the ease
with which you delve into
yourself

TRAINS

trains run on emotion not
good advice. the southern pacific
runs on a wet appetite. the trans-
siberian is loaded with boxes filled
with the tears of russians
going to hell. romanian rail-
roads run only in the rain and not
every time. on french
trains women give birth. and the rails
themselves are licked shiny every-
day by the tongues of museum
curators.

LOOKS FROM MONEY

ah, money, you colorless flat shit growing
from the uniqueness of this day like a grandmother
out of the pear tree,
what kind of dreadful holes are you boring
in the small of my back

money touched by gary cooper and by adolph hitler
oh money in balloons
take your hair out of my life broth
out with your guts and be gone

there is a train filled with blind birds
going broke

breasts fall from broken piggybanks
contracts are drawn in the park and photography
lays waste my mind

my bruised neck
in a thousand billfolds

CHORUS

a chorus is being organized
by something in my blood. i've sat
through endless rehearsals. the music
revolves around the word "OUT"
repeated ten thousand times with
everything i got. until
an audience is found
this setup will not work. there is no
room to sit any people unless
they agree to hang by their heads
from the cross in my crotch.

A SERIOUS MORNING

being serious is a
perversion of natural form
an extension of a bruised baby hand
behind which towers the tilted needle
of a dim father's body.
and the bees of his eyes dying with contempt.
i'm awash with the serious tools
of a mysterious trade.
the hushed windows of my receding house.
the power lines humming death wishes.
the dry wines in the palm of the hand.
if i were to laugh my ass off at all this
i would take up
a form of politics that ends
with a cheerleader licking the wounds
of my machine gunned body

THE POLICE

they are stripping the fur of the police
with these two eyes of mine.
a handful of witnesses bathe in wine
and the nymphlings shriek.
this is a scene from "history"
where it often happens that inside one's genes
is lodged a horror of police
like a horror of cats.
on which side of my emerging beard
should i start to stir?
oh right here. here is a place of
fur flakes, soft like your ass.

is this cavemoist making new bones?
until resurrection no one knows.
i like it that way.

SILENCE AT THE TOP

the silence of the dead trying to get up and shave!
the silence of the cold instrument
on the cold skin!   perception
of something brought to my door in the darkness
of a strange winter, a sum of cold
collected from the dead, a tool
for measuring love at the request of a tyrannical book,
a definitive form.   these then are the farms
in which the cattle of agreement are raised
by servants of the state, the barn
of the starless night hanging from a correct answer
like a scorpion from a slab of marble

THE IMAGINATION OF NECESSITY

there comes a time when everything is laced
the water you drink   the words you speak
your manner of speaking   of being
& the substance
is undefinable   coloratura of a
scale moving backwards into embryo tonality

which is not so bad when you possess a technique
of encounter or a professional philosophy
when you are a baker or an expert
lover   which is terrible when you live
with a rope around your neck a flower in your cock
a windlike disability   a flight pattern
drawn in the wrong sky in the wrong season
ducks sucked out of migration into disarray
oh concentrate then!   if you can
on the mystery ingredient   imagine your body
a spoon stirring the sugar at the bottom of a vast
cup of tea & the melting strings of sugar
on which the angels of hot water
climb with ferocious aptitude   what this imagining
gives   besides a headache   is an ease
of penetration a fluidity in entering strange
houses   a lack of weight in taking what's not yours
but fits you   & good luck

FROM

THE HISTORY OF THE GROWTH OF HEAVEN

(1973)

FACE PORTRAIT

"What will his crimes become, now that her hands have gone to sleep?"   John Ashbery

———————————————————

US

Oh I believe that all of us real poets string pickers
all of you great geniuses of my changing crystals
all of you and all beasts
have been growing hungry from a fast in us.
Now now here is the presence of mind
needed to stand up in the refrigerator and turn on the light
spouting from the butter, eerie eggs
of mind presence snowing near the gardens.
Dear God, Cauliflower & Broccoli are so Beautiful Together!
And the frozen ducks in the cracked cellophane pushing
a slice of pizza into the side of a clam can!
And the cheese singing!
Oh I believe that all of us
are ready!

FACE PORTRAIT

I am a man of face like another is "a man
of position" or "a man of hair." I take
things at their face values and the weight

of this world slides off
my face like a skier over snow. I live
through my face like others "get through
the day." It is not a particularly handsome
face, rather a gross sensual
barrage meant to take the breath out of you.
I imagine death as an epiphany of my face
in which a glow of dying roses clutched
in a diffusion of angles by discarnate hands
descends upon my eyes
and breaks them loose.
While the garters of divine ladies
snap and escape with my ears.
Still, I am alive and in this season of my face
there is the joy of sinning without surgery!

NEW YORK

The streets of this strange metropolis. . .
Frozen spaghetti, fear of ghosts. . .
The scarred pavements
have an eloquent texture
of bums woven with empty bottles and soot,
an ancient tapestry.
On this curious mattress one bounces looking for sex.
Layers and layers of sex
for each layer of you. . . Tongue overlaps
with ten thousand other tongues,
genitals are enmeshed in so many other genitals
that a ball of flame floats permanently around the city.
If you think this is rough
you don't know the heart of it because it's
silky and funny and feels
like the breeze of hereafter

A GRAMMAR

i was dead and i wanted peace
then i was peaceful and not quite dead yet
then i was in my clothes
and i took them off and then
there was too much light
and night fell
then i wanted to talk to somebody
and i spoke ecstatically
and i was answered on time in every language
in a beautiful way
but i felt unloved and everyone
came to love me

still there is something running
and i can't catch it
i am always behind

THE BEST SIDE OF ME

tomatoes squashes and cauliflowers intrigue me immensely
with their lewd proposals
and their making the stability of my appetite burst
with the lust of their red yellow and white chewiness.
you're chewy, i'm loooney.
i dream of soft furry things with inward claws
lodged in my brain
which open when it rains.
then whole cities built around a globe of waving squash.
we float backwards into early tickles of consciousness.
faces pull through complicated threads of greasy smiles.
my friend peter chewing on his model airplane.

the stretched frown of my tomato nanny.
if i ever walk out of this dream
my work is all over. my body releases
the captives from ten thousand labors.

SEA SICKNESS

dancers strapped to canoes is
what the morning brings. they are tied
to a perpetual dance.
hooded folks in lighthouses
count on their fingers as the day
gets brighter. everywhere
dancing is either law
or crime. i have no particular
taste for this world. i am looking
for an utterly still completely
dead hotel.

More

Opium for Britt Wilkie

The beautiful swimmer the extremely shy
opium eater touches his hat
in homage to the great pool lying
still at the feet of the crow. The
snow on his hat says
something to me but I am a weapon
with a small vocabulary
hanging from a deer horn rack. And
then he plunges into the blue water into
our afternoon. Oh hello there. We are
squeezing a string of smoke to cause our melo-
dramatic hearts to ripple up and down
the spine of the world. But he just
swims on sending a slight metallic shock
through us. OK. When we meet
again he will be swimming back having
brought a big wet clock with him from the other
side of this home

MANIFESTO

It's opium we need not truth.
Unless we are and we are morally pinned to the wall
with a gold stake. I am
pinned to your forehead, Karl Marx, like a
butterfly to a skirt.
The one way out is through blood, your
blood. Here, surrounded by the serenity
and transparence of opium
we sail toward the island of your blood.
When we stop we experience night.
As we go on the light of day bathes us.

ALBERTA

When Alberta swims the whole night in the creek behind
the house where I sit counting the rooms I want to
send owls in the branches above her with the results
of my count. 13 rooms, Alberta, 13 rooms! Or maybe
a thousand! But what owls, indeed what beasts, can last
the impact of her smooth, wet body leaving a trail of
warm dark men in the phosphorescent water . . . Two fishes
mate in the depression between her breasts! Waiting
their turn, all the other creatures in the creek are
emanating a light that messes up my count. How many
rooms did I say? Then she speaks from my faucet when
I drink and the glass of water in my hand shimmers with
an invisible lust. At the end of all these rooms, at
the end, indeed, of all rooms, there is Alberta swimming
on and her strokes inside my bloodcells culminate in
light, in small blue explosions.

Opium for Archie Anderson

I am home eating a heart A very slow
heart! A languishing pregnancy
pushes its lazy baby through the tenth
year! We hear the news under-
water Morsel after morsel
of hysteria Look I am home with the
bride She is lying
on a bed of artichokes with her heart hovering
over her overripe belly And
she hasn't been speaking for years except
to me! And
I lie! I lie a lot! I will
eat this heart I will go out and tell Look
I ate a heart I will
do it again! I will
eat your heart if only you could
be seized with such miracles! If only
you could rot so graciously on a bed
of artichokes If only you could
drive me south! Drive me deaf! If
you could bubble like mineral waters! If you
could walk up my ladders! Human
ladders!

Architecture

"Why not call it Egypt?"—Dick Gallup

Your public hair is the apex of a lovely
triangle rising through each day of my life

to complete a pyramid being secretly built
in my blood.
The mythical import of this construct
is then placed in the perspective of what the dead
are building under the streams, in what
imitations of us are being plotted by governments
in the cheaper materials, in rawhide
and in silver telephones

YOUR FANTASTIC OUTLINES

your fantastic outlines, inlines, mines and hollows
drop through my aroused pools
like heat sinking through the thermometer
of charlie manson's heart. revelation
of the love of being here.
this book of love will be written
out of the sheer propelling of my body into
those parts of you where foreign people drive
heavy trucks into the night of the best
love poems ever. but new. but best. but free
of mild chances, of robberies of love. free
of you even
as we float upstream
slipping
into the core of another element

Moments of Absolute Truth

When the gods die
the myths
are lifted off our backs
Peace be with them.
They were heavy.

Tom Clark

THE GOOD SPIRIT

the spirit of this room is dead. it was a very good spirit.
it kept the tea warm and it put me to sleep.
it fastened our love and it took good care of the heart.
it shone over the lower east side.
1 A.M.: things are unveiled, we are unprotected at night
and i want to plant an insane bomb in my own liver.
so i will never meet my edges again.
if only this disgust would leave me alone.

WHY WRITE

i've always looked for joy as a pretext to write
but could not or would not
fall face down upon that knot of pain which seems
to make even the simplest things
a complete and frightening mystery.
this way i have avoided being torn
by the terrific closeness with that heart-shaped weapon

which makes us die. i have left out
important fragments of my life. i've taken only
the juice out of the squalor. i have avoided
loving more than i *could* love.

EUGENIO MONTALE IN CALIFORNIA

and here where a new life
sprouts into a mild
anxiety from the orient
your words, like the scales on a dying fish,
flash into sunset

FEAR

fear is my way
of not being here although
i am afraid of falling asleep for fear
of a frightening thing taking place in my absence.
i am also
afraid of the axe i keep behind the bed hoping
that no one will come in or rather
that someone will
and there will be blood.
sitting there in the dark seeing myself kill
over and over
is not fear,

it is pleasure
though when the awareness of pleasure floats up
and i learn that it is pleasure
i become very afraid.
this new house is fear
of the unknown neighbors stretching for miles
in each direction with only
space for houses with no one in them
space for dark windows over basements filled with fear.
the long stone walk from the door
to the top of the stairs
has three major checkpoints of fear:
the cottage on the right where the spooks sit
on the bicycle chains,
the old jew's apartment with the curtains drawn
over the candle light
and finally the stairs themselves going up
through minor and major stations of fear
which at the age of six are like the days themselves,
long, inexorable.
and now the fear of even writing about fear
the fear of awareness

POEM

the supreme test of one's poem
is in the bathtub standing up naked hands
above the head like a gothic christ
and if the picture in the mirror is of a fat
belly swaying between the forks of a black grin
it's still OK! but no poem

Alice's Brilliance

Her brilliance consists in colors. She can sink her teeth into a nuance from one thousand steps like the Lone Ranger. She sees rainbows, desert sunsets and Dutch Boy factories in every drop of water and in this tablecloth. There is nothing doesn't come to her for therapy because she can, you see, cure grey desperate people by yanking the veil from their eyes and revealing the brilliant dazzle even in the patches of their pants. Everyone is richer for her presence. Since she came to town we move more graciously, there is coquetry in the air, the trees bow gallantly. *I don't want to upset my colors over you, buster,* says the traffic cop handing out a rolled papyrus with a ticket written on it in gold ink and gothic characters. His pearl-handled revolver sways gently on his curved hip. The old truckdrivers even exude an air of civilization, a think blanket of pink. All the rougher colors gather by the river and tell violet stories shifting their eyes like needles in the ochre light. At times her brilliance attains peaks of perfection and we feel pierced by unknown and unnamed colors that then stay perched like vultures on our hearts and defend us against death.

TALISMANIC CEREMONY FOR LUCIAN, MARCH 9, 1971, INTERSECTION CHURCH, SAN FRANCISCO

since he's not jewish
and he won't get circumcised
or bar mitzvahd

since he's not christian
and he won't get christened
or given first communion

since he's not a baby anymore
and too big to wear
pink and blue pajamas

i now pronounce him a kid

this is a solemn ceremony
in which
his mommy
is giving him back
his umbilical cord

to protect him from this world
with a talisman
from another

this is then a solemn ceremony
in which
his father
is giving him a new name

LUCIAN CODRESCU

to make him the first

FROM

GRAMMAR & MONEY

1973

&

i hate
everything that moves faster than my body because
everything that moves faster than my body
does so by a cheap trick

DESIGNS

the zodiac towel wipes the hands
of the zodiac killer
and burns up. the zodiac towel
was designed by peter max. the
zodiac killer was designed by god.
both of them, god
and max, are prefigured
in the zodiac
as very great designers

THE WORST POEMS MAKE THE BEST "POEMS"

If my manner of song disturbs the dead the living
and the near dead it is because
near the dead end you can't dance.
I dance to the noise of market places and to the jingle
of coins in the pocket of a subway cop
I dance with the quiver of tomatoes
slipping into paper bags
and I dance to the tune of a day when I will be dead
and the farts of a cow near my tomb
will drive me bots

FROM

Secret Training

(1973)

ON ORGANIZATION

Has anyone ever earned the respect of sand?
Cement has.
Anything that can be organized can be made
to respect the organizer.
Organization is the process whereby the organizer
eats the organizable.
Anyone with a big stomach can be an organizer.
Only the undigestible is unorganizable.
Therefore make thee as horrible to eat as boiled
spinach!

DREAM

They operated on my brain. First she cut a round slice off the top of my head and put it aside then she extracted a big piece of brain from the front. She put the top back on and notwithstanding my fears of memory loss she told me to come back next day. In the hallway outside I meet their beautiful daughter who is a dancer. Next day I come back to have my brain piece reinserted. I am given a shot and the top of my head is again cut off. Last night's fresh brain looks refrigerated, an old piece of liver. "IS THIS MY BRAIN?" I gasp. "IT WILL FRESHEN UP AGAIN ONCE IT'S BACK INSIDE YOUR HEAD" she says; they put it back inside my head and they sew the top on. Today I am feeling very weird, very fragile like somebody had stuck the arm of a compass into the center of my head and traced a circle just above the eyebrows.

The Urges

When the urge to strip becomes too much i rub against a tree until it passes back into that core of myself where, beside stripping, urges such as bashing someone's head in, lie still waiting for signs to proceed. Every day i look for incidents. My heart is a bomb with a very fine trigger. Sometimes a hair falls on my nipple and BOOM! the desire to strip or kill is loose and, look out, i've got my eye on you. Rubbing against trees is my only defense against myself. I smell like bark and there is a rustle of leaves when i pass.

Power

Power is an inferiority complex wound up like a clock by an inability to relax. At the height of my power I have to be taken to a power source in the woods where I am recharged. This power source is not actually in the woods: it's in my mother. It hums quietly in her heart like an atomic plant and the place to plug in is her eyes.

Silence

The town is never silent. No matter what time it is there is always someone talking. And if no one was talking the wires alone are enough to wake the dead. When the dead wake, forget about silence! All those rattling bones! And even if the people, the wires and the dead were silent, there would still be the indefinite hum of the blood in all the bodies in all the houses. And this is where I come in with my mouth full of silence. I am the size and the shape of an atomizer filled with silence and when I squeeze my inner springs a jet of spray coats everything with the shiny lacquer of silence. In this way I resemble snow but I am more like a self-conscious singer.

De Rerum Natura

I sell myths not poems. With each poem goes a little myth. This myth is not in the poem. It's in my mind. And when the editors of magazines ask me for poems I make them pay for my work by passing along these little myths which I make up. These myths appear at the end of the magazine under the heading ABOUT CONTRIBU-TORS or above my poems in italics. Very soon there are as many myths as there are poems and ultimately this is good because each poem does, this way, bring another poet into the world. With this secret method of defying birth controls I populate the world with poets.

FOR MAX JACOB

(1974)

BI-LINGUAL

I speak two languages. I've learned one of them in a trance, for no reason at all, in a very short time, on horseback, in glimpses, between silent revolts. One is the language of my birth, a speech which, more or less, contains my rational mind because it is in this tongue that I find myself counting change in the supermarket and filing away my published poems. In a sense, these two languages are my private day and night because what one knows without having learned is the day, full of light and indelicate assumptions. The language of the night is fragile, it depends for the most part on memory and memory is a vast white sheet on which the most preposterous things are written. The acquired language is permanently under the watch of my native tongue like a prisoner in a cage. Lately, this new language has planned an escape to which I fully subscribe. It plans to get away in the middle of the night with most of my mind and never return. This piece of writing in the acquired language is part of the plan: while the native tongue is (right now!) beginning to translate it, a big chunk of my mind has already detached itself and is floating in space entirely free...

LES FLEURS DU CINÉMA

i would like to throw a net over these moments when i find myself in the position of an accountant, a clerk of the world, in order to capture them for a future window display of objectivity, a box of signatures from a perfectly harmonious space. these moments like certain flowers bloom so rarely that the entire being of the world participates in their detection. cinema is the great fertiliser. often i find myself in a perfectly dark movie theatre being swiftly seized by an involvement with objective substance until the chair under me melts and there, on the vast cinemascope screen, i hear myself breathing a variety of numbers, all perfect, all accurate, all full of the sweetness of the absolute. this casket of numbers inside which my clear body will never decay is then taken out through a hole in eastman kodak into the mind of god whose fodder these bodies are. and that's that.

Evening Particulier

What did you eat? Who did you call? Oh, exquisite asparagus, I lift these tatters of myself to the sorrows of the alphabet and despair of ever being as splendid as you! Neither will I ever be like a piano! Or like an onion! Imagination is my grace and I am tired of her constant presence!

PORT OF CALL

did you ever have a grey knot topped symbolically with lightning bolts and mounted in the middle of yourself like a pagoda? of course not. but i have. i have the only one in the world or rather i had because i've traded it in for a scarf. this scarf is from god. you can see smears of cheese on it. cheese? yes, god's feet are made of cheese. wherever he walks he leaves smears. that's how he walked upon the waters . . . the water went into the holes in the cheese and the whole thing swole up . . . like floaters . . . rubber balloons. except that they were cheese shoes. the cheese shoes of jesus. well, anyway, that's how i got the scarf, but i will trade it to you for a paddle board. do you need a paddleboard? no, but i know someone who does . . . he'll trade his gum wrappers for the paddle board. do you need gum wrappers? no, i will give the gum wrappers to a tall man . . . he knows me. he wants the wrappers because he needs to wrap himself. do you need anything? yes. i need a port of call.

Mail

Envelopes arrive from everywhere and they are filled with earth. In the beginning I suspected that this was a holy sort of ground which, when possessed in large quantity, would allow me to kneel on it and plant a few vegetables. It is nothing but sand. It has the appearance of fertile earth but after a few days it turns to sand. All the drawers and the closets are filled with sand. What disconcerts me is the night which brings with it the sound of the sea as if the great waters were looking for a lost beach. I sleep in my clothes.

FROM

The Marriage of Insult and Injury
(1977)

BODY BLUES

What do you body want? Food? Food?
Here, body, have some food. What does
the body want? Coffee? Coffee? Here here
body have some coffee! Outside? Outside?
Let's go! Inside? Pussy? Pussy?
Here body have some pussy! Movies? Movies?
Here here body there there. Didn't you
get enough tit? Why didn't you? What was
the matter with her? Pushups?
Pushups? I'm pushing you up and down
body, what do you want now?
Speak, goddammit!

CASTING

My clothes grow dull in the closet.
The men in them grow restless like the sea.
The man in the blue suit is hungry. He walks across
the menu like a lion, hitting his gabardine reflection
in the window on the neck with a blue glove.
An intelligent romantic fills my chinese kimono.
His violence, curled like a mandrake at the bottom of a tea cup,
is poised to strike a flying spirochete: an angel.
In my shoes stands the crowd, fresh back from war,
striking for softer roads.
On them falls the shadow of my trousers like a sword
as the silk fold of the night milks itself in a new way.
But I am standing naked, on a rock face, in the moon.

This is my perfect balcony and with the loaf
of French bread in my hand I am now pointing
at the chasm below, where a vast and hideous
animal is hiding: Eat! You mutha! I flex a rubber arm.
This animal, a rich relation, incurring both hope and horror,
swims up: it is the Hat.
Yes, consider simply the business of buying a hat
if you think words get born in a fog:
between the man who buys a hat and the man
who is afraid of his hair
a chasm opens filled with the bodies of a thousand
awkward thinkers, bad athletes, men not ready.
You may look wistfully toward the other side
watching with ill-concealed envy the tall door
closing behind the stark gentleman.
Maybe, one day, you tell your head.
Maybe one day when the lumps in you and the lack
of hair will make the leap inevitable,
maybe then I too will stand under the yellow lamplight
on the rain-wet sidewalk to tell a lonely
war veteran hurrying in his wheelchair toward god-knows
what awful supper in the deserted city:
I have joined the bourgeoisie! I can go home now!
which will or will not be sufficient.
You tell your head all these things: the Hat
glows in the window of the chasm below. It has no feelings
so you walk endlessly around its rim.
Without the hat
they will never shoot you for the boredom you bear in your heart!
With the hat, the man in the blue suit will get to eat.
With it, the intelligent romantic will find the mirror
on which he'll squash his angel flat.
With it, the crowd will get to grow fat.
Without it, they will make guerrilla war.
Well, hat or no hat?
So I am naked on a jutting rock.
It would help if I remembered who wore it and when:

then my head would shake my hand and together
we would begin walking up the broken mosaic
of the overgrown path toward the music
where we would be greeted—by the bandstand—with the news
that night has closed up the armories
and we are out of weapons.

To My Heart

I am a cross and the idea
Is to burn twice at the four tips.

All night I work the hoses putting
Out fires in-between.

The fires I understand are vices and
The idea comes from my heart

Threatening to stop.
It beats six times and then it leaps

Upward into nothingness. It feels
Like a rehearsal.

I better stop smoking, drinking and rocking
Little dogs on my lap.

I see somebody bigger than the moon
Delve into my affairs.

Somebody's making a mistake.
I may be talking fast but I am only

28 years of age.
Some day I will be all the rage.

The Life on Film of St. Theresa

She carefully wrapped an egg in each sock
of the martyr who died of shock.
She tied them around her neck, and was wandering.
One day she bled at an inn, in the snow.
The air was pierced by arrows of Ave Maria, sudden
flurries of wings. Open the bound encyclopedia,
and let me into the brown sky, mother of god, she cried.
A frozen woman under an icicle basked in simplicity.
The book opened: in it, the Savior was squeezed tight
twixt Salad and Savoir. Still, there was room in Heaven.
She arrived at his side on the pinpoint of her emotions.
Two large circles of sweat danced around her shoulders.
She saw from there things big indeed, and cherished.
The snow is awake, clouds loom, wars break in print,
she cried, and I am full oh beasts called Past & Light,
of an animal love, and I see, at all times, a great
furry animal loving me, with the same passion!

The Yes Log

Say Yes to all and be condensed in fact!

Poems are sermonettes for all the interlocking
tremors in the land.

The brain turns toward its great surprise
like a revolving door holding
a giant red ant
                    Surprised?
It rains with gusto.

What are we doing here with the recipe for father?

Take two parts sand and one part ladder.
Mix with parsley, fry and scatter.

And then say Yes to the precisely knotted whip
which lashes
down your succession and up your ancestry,
so that in touching
each past or future face it can
change you from shit to gold?

O stamp of hell o electricity!

The Question of Personnel

Glorious summer day! Clump of hot rocks!
I am naked looking at the vulture heading down
for my aspirin bottle! (Vultures get
these immense headaches from so much blue)
These rocks are an anchor, else I'd be up there with you.
I would sail for an encore anywhere.
The eyes of a thousand skinny runts are focused on me.
If he can do it, they say, why can't we.
I'm not about to do it, I'm too attached to my aspirin.
It would be good to walk up to the medicine cabinet
on a fine day for the ego and say to the aspirin bottle:
Eat my ass! It's the best thing going these days!
and then firmfingered grab it by the childproof cap
and throw it to the vultures.
Ah, then I'd be up there to congratulate the father
of Creative Jive!
Lord, I would say, forgive us our hidden intentions
even if they are clear to you.

It is our clarity, I know, that baffles you.
I know that as I explain myself my state of mind rivals
that of the angels.
Then I would begin to embroider:
I have worked, Sir, on this quilt for 30 years.
I am in the middle of it and with your permission
I would like someone else to finish it.
It is this half a forest with lean unicorns
fucking each other in a grove of fir
and all my successor has to do is put
a little more love into it and a couple of soda-
fountains so that everyone will know it was made in America.
My intuition does not side with a vast burst of nonsense.
In Heaven embroidering is a dignified occupation.
The rinse in the wine glass foams in Double O Crochet
on the lips of the assemblage.
The Termite is taking her siesta, the house is no more.
A faded man shines in a novel.
From the mind rises the Paragraph.
The years lift like the inches of skirt above the knees
but there is barely any urgency to time.
All things it seems are grateful and fair
to the wall through which the chronometer ticks.
Hot rocks! Summer day! The girls go by
smuggling flutes into the trumpet section.
Sans vulture, the sun, where it sits, cloaked in causality,
is a Seurat of tiny monks taking their pillows to heaven.

THE DIFFERENCES
for Barbara Szerlip

When it comes to sentiment, as it will, you can't compete
with the bourgeoisie, or with the radio.

*

It says, on my diploma: sheer irresponsibility with a touch of cruelty: the man is licensed to practice.

*

I'm really shy
and deep
inside
i don't give anyone the eye
enter the
      nude
    bride
       descending
  the spiral
      staircase

*

On their knees, people say funny things. I always tell them: You will speak normally, when you recover!

*

One more inch and you're out of a job!

*

If a fleeting impression is the whole performance, the fact of something nameless enters the body of the fierce yolk, endlessly urging the egg to scramble itself.

*

You are intelligent, my heart goes out to you.

*

The trees may be scary
but hidden among them
is your house

I am St. John the Baptist, my work heralds the birth of
Jesus.

*

Future delights are an attack on their sources: only miracles
are relevant.

*

You got somethin horrible
And God said that you must die
So you turn to poetry
And begin to cry-eeee

*

There is economy in the unconscious. The horses of Apocalypse
are on a ration of hay. Heaven is not running out of miracles
but there are fewer Distributors.
I am offering you a job.

The degenerate
vampire

haunts the out-
skirts of the hemo-
philia camp

*

The man is a woman, the woman is a man, their child is
silent between them like the lights of a strange city
underlining the vast differences.

*

She lived in a bottle of Black & White, he lived in her
closet. Their children, the blackbirds, swooped down on
them in the winter, and flew away in V flocks, their feathers
staying behind as pillows, mementoes.

*

The employment of difference is not a big business, the
universe looks with indifference at evolution.

*

He refused to let them cover his eyes
and as the volley began
he shouted:
vive la différence!

*

The devil's sense of humor spawned photorealism while
impressionism tended to favor god.

*

The objective observer lay his rifle on the wrong side
of generalization, and sleep took him apart like a watch.

*

Daytime, an arbitrary variety of.

*

Degeneracy is the fruit of sympathy. Us healthy animals
we like to kick ass.

THE PARK

What is recorded
does not lack passion, standing power or suspense,
yet where does this rage spring from that mows
the people down and bleeds the cows?
If any process, any flowing thing
is really nothing,
if the night is really nothing,
where does this hysteria, this great compulsion
to witness a basic sadness,
come from?
Do I pull myself by conclusions like an elevator
or is this, simply,
boredom by the flowers?

A victim of lively interest and constant bending.

How can I close the window or the book and be
alone with the torrential
manners of my skin? How keep
the claws half-out, the icepacks half within?

If only, as I write, the words would get obscene.
If only they would stand on their long legs
and turn
their full nakedness on me
like spotlights

sucking dead birds and prisons out of darkness.

What could, without foreclosure, audits and ruins,
warm this heart and offer
completeness to the brain?

Mint, parsley, violets and dandelions?

Is there a private park around here
to know the name of and then
roll on its views?

SPACE SOUFFLÉ

There is only content
pleading "no contest" to the cracked egg
of energy, lifting itself out of parents
into Paris where they are waiting
with candles and champagne

What are they waiting for while loving
the content of their hands?

The universe, which is a hero's welcome,
is merely a description
to be waited on, day and night,
with one foot always in the air

The lovers of the Air Force line the streets,
watching their loved ones fill the sky
with energy, and crashing into towers

The contents spill
so that this night won't be forgotten

Head trapped by seeds and helicopters

Old Cities

The contentment is seen at the tip. I am so
anxious to see the little light and win.
But it is tipped off by the rain, the little light,
and by the lane that ends ahead.
I should get angry but I get sad.
In other cities, at other times, the little light
was everywhere. I couldn't sit in buses
because it burned the seat. Those are, perhaps,
its cities and the buses
are where it lives.
Will they, when I return, return my light?
Or will I hit my center at the moment
I discover it gone? And in that hit I will see water.
I chase my light with buckets of black water.

A Textual Recording

In other words, it is the conspiracy of the I
and the he, first and third persons, who
merge toward you.

He is composed of thousands of he's hanging
in the air above the world which is
the main subject.

The he closest to I
reaches down and with an enormously long hand
grabs a hold of the world
through the eyes of I.

I turns around then upside down and catches
the flying ground to reach
you
who is busy in the world.

I reaches within to catch you
take you out of the world

up to he
who can show you the better views
from the air

so that you can walk down from the highest he
into the lowest, hanging barely
above the world

and with his fresh enthusiasm, like a long
hand,
reach below and grab the I

SADNESS UNHINGED
for Dubcek

A faded man shines in a novel
like a Jew in a 1943 photo.
There are
translucent sands that nurse the step along:
Where are you going?
You I will nurse along for not remembering.
I hurt. At the back of my head, a hand
pushes the skull inward.
I have lost the sense of my life.
I am cold sober.

I see the stove and I count the bullets in the revolver.
A hand has pulled from the inside
all that made firmness firm,
the velvet without the valuable,
the gut of the balloon,
the air.
I am of an intricately flawed quality,
my gourds are singed, I will not tamper with the river.
I am a dog, lost in the dark, lonely, cold and humid cement
cell of the Humane Society,
waiting for my owners who will not come.

*

My despair like this poem
comes only once.
My terror is constant.
I live with the forked ends
of a formal victory.
I live without a tent.
I am not satisfied with ambiguity,
it takes two of them to get me off.
Duality often, out for a swim,
drowns in ambiguity.
I sustain joy in the mortality
of the hair, or the green section.
Nothing is too extreme
for my erection.
Why not, like this erection,
tend only to your own beliefs?
Imitate your cocks,
you foolish heads!
Girls, find your own metaphors.
Imitate your cocks
the heads of which light
the way; there are prisms
buried in them, diamonds cutting
their way out of museums, cubes
of light singing navels to sleep.

If you imitate well
I will let you out of Hell.
The light in Hell is sick.
The sign MOTEL flickers on and off.
Tiny bluebeards carry silver coffins
with rococo handles.

Everyone around me is dying.
But not the ones I love.
A warped sentimentality begins
to take apart the barn.
Will the cow stand the rain?
Death stalks the bushes
in Santa Barbara.
My friend JR bids me look at his gun,
a thing out of Dostoievsky whom
many of you will be reading again,
and says: "With this, I'll check out."
There is no air, only endless
luggage counters in sterile terminals.
Pain racks his body and he throws
the morphine out the window
like Coleridge, and I weigh the gun, say:
"You mind waiting until
I get out of the room?
I hate a mess."
"But the world," said he,
"if that's a mess,
how can you stand it?"
The distance between realities is anyone's guess,
and what grows on it, less and less.

One kindergarten child, alone, trudges up hill carrying
a whole forest under his arm.
They gave it to him in school.
When I was a child, a faded child in an old country,
in a poor school, in a poor country,
learning was the pleasure of watching Something come out of
Nothing; not paper, certainly.

You, American kindergartener, are taking home the body
of your mother, her pubic hair. What are you going to do
when you get home, and she is not there?
Oh, child, I am so sorry. But what happened to you?
Why are you so tall, of a sudden? Why do your shoulders
have basketball hoops? Why does your T-shirt say
HOMO AMERICANUS, in letters as large as the clouds?

A Cook in Hell

1.

As I was going whistling down the hill of Hell
I saw a man shitting through the top of his head:
there was a hole like a bell and through it came
the golden turds, and other matters dead.
Half human and half porcelain, these beings filled the sky.
Have they golden intelligence? Or are they acrobats
composing the fetid ritual of an ancient dawn? I said
to myself, upon spotting so many more, everywhere.
Priests, whores, acrobats, charmers, all convinced
by the well placed brown rose at the top of their hair,
launched their canoes into the higher air,
as uncontrolled and joyous as a barrel full of nymphs.
Sighing, I continued my descent, down the singular
lane with its peculiar beauty, of slaughtered innocents
planted like peanut trees in the black sand,
watching me with poisoned envy, turning every bend.
On this road I saw a woman trudging up hill away from
what must be the inconceivable basements of Hell,
and two children trudged after her, and a husband.
As we pass, she points a long pointed index
at the direction I am going in, relentlessly obsessed,

and says: "I like your direction better than mine"
and I'm rooted to the spot, uncomprehending, to say:
"You always can, my house is Thine!"

2.

She leaves her life and follows me, back on the road to Hell.
There is a stand along the road, a shiny, modern kitchen.
She hangs the shopping bag from a hatrack which also is a hand
that sorts meat from cheese and parsley root from pepper bell,
and sits in a rotunda, overlooking a yellow ocean self-possessed
to a metallic point, and sand dunes full of skulls marked "Sell,"
while I boil purple water in which a fetus swims or seems to jell
and chop the huge mushrooms we have called "Hats," both for
        their
size as well as for their politeness to the knife.
They are hats for very large heads these meats of which
the dirt is rife, these ancient sprouts of wisdom and these harsh
citizens of moss-filled bogs and caves and swamps,
the heads of, say, Saint Francis or Pascal, heads known
to be both large and filled with thoughts and serial complaints.
I pray, as I bring down the knife, that there are no heads inside
these hats; I pray also that in the coming night
shade will not stray from us; and finally I pray that every slice
will be noted, and recorded, not once or twice, but thrice.
But heads they are because this is the road to hell.
Au revoir, Saint Francis, I didn't mean to faint the balcony.
Their tears owe their sublime to your pain, not my ignorance.
Adieu, Pascal, you can love your God now!
If I had not just now killed them how would they have died
        for you?
The cook must invest in pain, he will be questioned about
        sorrow
not happiness, or joy, or rain. He is not protected by a wall
of glass bearing the fingerprints of the working class, as are
the artichoke hearts, already torn out of the artichokes.
He is alone in a field of slaughter which he would like to close.
A hundred souls, awake, supervise his activity, and buzz.

If he yielded for a second to look at these extraordinary bees
of the departed, into their sunken eyes, he would find himself
at the bottom of a valley, among twisted propellers,
he would perceive the future with a groan, a howl and a sigh,
as a continuous, hysterical, subterranean, snaky and avuncular
Revolt, spreading under the ground to the potatoes, to the lily
bulbs, to the onions, and to the carrots, rousing them
from tubercular somnolence and roasting them to vicious fury,
rocketlike, in the first fireworks on the outermost rim of Hell.
There is a blindness they approve of in the name of Homer, here.
They say, on little braille tablets nailed to maimed orphans,
that the blind feel good in a thousand obscure ways, and that
the place of the cook is to use his kitchen knife for proportion
and not for surgery because Davis Pharmaceutical is in that
        business,
and furthermore, that the absence of sharp cuts whets the
        appetite.
That is what they say, and I am keeping a blue line of restraint
when suddenly I feel a boiling in my blood as if the tent
of my entire life were just right now collapsing on some floor,
and I want to enter, with my cock, into the hollows and the
        creases
of each legume, animal and essence, and get past the outer shell.
To the last moment, the cook must be in readiness to bring
the last joyful asparagus in the world to a standstill with a blow
on the thinnest neck at the base of the stalk, thus closing
a fair chapter in the history of the race, and opening
the window to an age of oil, a wave of which will spell to all
that thus pass the days and still no soup.

3.

And so a time there comes when one must move, and get his bag
of trinkets, to continue the steep descent below the dreamer's pits.
All around him, there are children, playing with an extraordinary
lack of awareness of either direction, or the nearness of Hell.

The woman, as they leave the kitchen, tells him that he must
either go up, back into the light he remembers so well, or they
must part, she having no intention of any further descent, and so
the tragic part is he so readily assents and everyone is getting
new ski boots, alpinists' tools, cans of rations, and a short
lecture on the ecstatic worlds of paradise, where in the freedom
of an eternal summer, the people and the trees share every meal.
As we were going thus whistling up and away from the hill of
        Hell
we passed a poet, much in need of food, and air, and clothing
and a great lack of say in the affairs of a demented world,
and as we passed, my woman of a whole fortnight, she said she
        liked
his direction better than hers, and together, they began what was
a brand new journey into Hell, a fresh descent and, knowing her,
in a fortnight, a brand new thrust for health, and trees, and air.

                    4.

The children, as the will would have it, are outlined
like trembling geese against the patchy snow of a bright day.
Only I know this brightness to be the lit halo of a saint and not
what peasants commonly mistake for day, a halo that is a
        circular
searchlight encompassing the bodies of the innocent in their
attic rooms reading with flashlights dirty books, and tending
to their erections, and their guitars, and their terrains,
a halo tuned to be both not too bright and not too dim, a perfect
lamp in the immenseness of the locked-up night.
But in ascending, you must pay a toll which is to turn this
        halo up
in passing, as if a nightmare guides your hand, and in so doing
you will light the world with a bright cobalt blue fierceness,
waking the children in the night, making them see themselves out-
lined in blood, with their erections, and razors crossing every
game they've played like a page, scarring them forever, and so
        hard
that they will always treat themselves to flight,
going from every little thing toward the safety of the night,

with pears and breasts burnt to a cinder, dancing in their eyes,
until the angels mercifully place baskets of fruit on their new
        graves.
All these heads framed in the harsh police light: I have
looked at all of them, Sir. The suspect is not in the line-up.
I could not turn that halo's beam on my own children so
I packed up their ropes, and tools, and back we went, toward the
depths of pure, unravaged Hell where, for the night we stopped
in the roadside kitchen, watching the poet cook a meal, for
there were now a full quire of us, and hungry too.

5.

His kitchen had decorum, as opposed to mine which was
a mess of things, a constant urging on, and then some other
        things,
having to do with pity, guilt and appetite undaunted.
His kitchen was like a court lined with satin pillows: in it
one was both judged, and made love to in impromptu positions.
The cooking went on with total regard for form, and the guests
all had staple guns with which they seemed to constantly
staple posters to each others' heads, announcing that the discord
of events would be solved in a place set apart for the purpose,
during a great burst of voice, by one or the other of those present.
The children loved the din, they thought it was music, and also,
on silver screens that slid directly into their hearts, they saw
movies of their own minds going into tail-spins, or getting born,
or solving problems that then shined, and splintered like mica.
Even their sleep, in this new kitchen, was made from the
        substance
of a thing apart from their dreams, from the dreams of others or
from the dreams of many anguished historical nights, or
        unknown,
it was a sleep like that of well-fed slaves who fell into the glass
of their own image, and then budged no more,
it was the sleep of slaves fed on philosophy, and dogs fed on
        time,
a sleep I should have whips for, when I pass.

And yet, like in my kitchen too of not so long ago, the nights
passed like the days, and still no food, and still
the distance steadily remained the same from Hell, and the view.
And to the children then I bid goodbye, who stood there saved
from cobalt light and burning halos, who stood there fusing
with strange life-forms, octopi and horses, outlined by the
        decorum
of the kitchen, surrounded by small flames, and literature,
who stood there like windows behind which the unhappy
        forefathers
strained their ghostly eyes, watching for a sign.
The depths of Hell were winking and again, I started for its
        lights.

6.

My birth, they tell me, is a house, and my destination is a store.
A strange mother this, sending me out for more, and more.
So on the road going through the woods, from my house to the
        store,
I call myself Animal, and am ready to act like one, or two,
should love appear, in the nude, with breasts, and nipples, and
maybe a scar or two, or a limp, or a distinctive swear, should
she appear out of nowhere, on the road through the trees through
which the town appears dimly, with flaming cupolas, and Exxon
        in
the night sky, should she appear now, together we might fly.
Certainly, elegance must be careful, and geometry stand up to
        lust.
But the trees mock me, the love I see doesn't last, there is only
        wind
and I am awkwardly dressed among these trees, which I feel
like cutting down, before I buy, from the store, bread, cheese,
and Oui Magazine, and a score of unrelated complexities, for
        mom.
Ah, but a pervading melancholy makes mushrooms the fashion
        in hats!
Ah, but for the mind from which rises the Paragraph!

I walk alone and I begin to slide but I am careful not to slip
on the downward slopes of Hell, on the shiny long trail with a
          prong
in Eternity, through which flows oil, and fluid materiel,
I am careful not to use the voice against itself to tell
jokes too horrible to hear, punchlines from which the laughter
          fell,
I'm careful, but in such a reckless way, God only knows and He
          is
off the air, as I walk alone through the Four Squeezes:
Squeezed between the pages of news, politics eats only raw heart.
Squeezed in the paraplegic's hook the bulb fits in the tricky
          socket.
It is getting worse for Jews and Americans.
Squeezed between the rise of professionalism and the
          mushrooming
of cheap feeding stations, the cook is fed to Madame La Mort.
Squeezed between bargains I feel that I am an opportunity
for civilization, and for what forms choose to remain when the
          devil
uncovers the pot, to see how it's cooking.
As I was going whistling down the hill of Hell
I saw that such forms were pure as chose to remain:
some flocked away when the blood slowed down,
others when the tiny umbrellas collapsed in the wet fields,
and others yet disappeared when the only razorblade in the
          universe
was found half-imbedded in the wrist of God, thus making it hard
to chop up the promised reward into the finest grain there is.
But others stayed to march into the flames with me, and be
consumed by both large and small fires, like criminals in joy,
skating on necessity, realized in speed, born in the heat
of a mother and father chasing each other around a lit dial.
Nothing was merely or yet human. Spring came, the ice melted,
through the holes in the clouds I saw figures and facts,
the wrong facts, the right figures, and then I saw my goal:
a pasture full of Gypsies riding their horses through the holes.
Under them, all of us were going on foot, pushing our bodies
through a huge, clean ear, through the flames of a wide ring.

I have no patience, said the President of Hell, with those
who do not pay precise attention to their present circumstances.
I can barely emphasize the danger!
And yet, all around him, extreme logic was in effect,
and yet, warmed by his voice we were jesters at the courts of
        Librium.
The master of Hell was a dinosaur on a couch, drawling out
the psychoanalysis of the paleolithic, posing for a picture by
Alice Codrescu, [c.] 1976, and dispensing advice to the free to
        hear.
To the one next to me he said: 'Push the furs aside,
and ask to see the Furrier!' To another, he advised, 'Go find
a lawn and start a revolution among the worms!' And to me, he
        said:
'Everywhere they are boarding the buses to work.'
'Sleeping securely when everyone is gone, is a luxury you do not
        have.'
'Not in a thousand years, not in your grave.'
'I think that you are ready to audition for the Night
and you might or you might not get a part!'
Before I could thank him, the world parted, and I was swimming
in a black river from the middle of which a rapid deep current
beckoned, and out of which a gruesome fish came and said:
'Audition in 10 minutes for all the bathers up stream!' of which
I was one. And surely, soon I drowned, with others but alone.
A number of them looked me over: not enough dark meat for
        the night!
Not enough protein for Hell! Back to the Day!
At this, I was forced upward suddenly, like a man in a geiser
        chair,
and I found myself climbing the slopes, away from Hell,
with a new view of things in which order was not essential
but the very next meal very much so, a new view from which, I
        must
tell, pride is missing, and only the shell of it all stays.
Of course, I stopped by the kitchen, half way up to tell
a number of cafe regulars of which you are one, that the director
of Hell adored me in secret, but sent me back for my friends.
When we go en masse, I will promise to better polish my tenses.
Until then, will art override the expenses?

FROM

THE LADY PAINTER

(1977)

The Penal Cavalry

QUIT PLAYING GAMES!
START FACING THINGS!
and then i stopped playing games
and i faced things
and all i could think of was
I WOULD LIKE TO WRITE A BOOK CALLED
"THE PENAL CAVALRY"
and this book was from the point of view
of someone who faced things
and this someone found that he couldn't
leave his room because each thing
he faced had a thousand faces
and staring into each one in turn
took a very long time
so one day he joined
THE PENAL CAVALRY
which was a way of facing things
at a fantastic speed
on top of a horse
and he found that facing things
this way
he could have
a little time for himself
a time in which he closed himself up like a shell
and faced nothing
for hours at an end

The Monk

I saw a fantastic description of a monk's cell. This monk made wine and one wall was lined with barrels and bottles while another held a wide bookshelf. In the middle was a solid oak table on which there was a lamp and variety of papers. The cell was in the woods and the woods were in the mountains on a gentle slope facing East. Everything the monk wrote he read to the trees and in the fall, when he made his wine, he poured some of it on their roots from big clay jugs. Every time I feel depressed I think about that monk and how, as long as there are trees, I can be just like him and then nothing depresses me any more.

Center Piece

I can't think of any man or woman without also thinking "poor man!", "poor woman!". This "poor" is a box I've created over the years. There is nothing inside it and this is precisely why it is my favorite creation. Even the walls of this box are made of nothing. I love to contemplate, when night falls, this box made of absolutely nothing with nothing inside, just sitting there in the middle of myself surrounded by so many things and by so much anxiety. It is always quiet when I become aware of it and if it wasn't for the fact of my mortal body I would enlarge it to contain the Universe.

TOWARD THE END OF 1969

suddenly toward the end of 1969 everything is
"objectified" after a fashion that leaves
you in your clothes but not in your mind
and every day sees
the birth of new instruments, wooden and
metallic, born out of circumstance, conjecture
and plain absence.   not to under-
estimate these things a new set of values
is also born and not only does one not under-
estimate but one praises
lavishly, completely, with the dedication
of a saint to the cross.   sets of
paternal and maternal perception knock
patiently at the doors of the brand new cubicles
like infant birds in eggs with a right
to this world but, really, what right
to my world does a cane, a shoe or a hat have
what right except part-time presence?
i wonder but it all comes to this: even i
see no wrong with the 90 per cent "alien-
ness" of the world and i
should know better because i
am a poet

Au bout du temps

So late in the 20th Century
    So late in the 20th Century
   At the end almost of the 20th Century
 I sit in my home
    In my modest and meaningless home
    And worry about my penis
   ABOUT MY PENIS FOR CHRISSAKES!

In praise of biology
  In praise of visions...
Only a few years ago it did not seem
   so late in the 20th Century
    it did not seem very late
     in the 20th Century
   this saddest of centuries
maybe the 14th was a very sad century
   fin de siècle
    mal de siècle
mal de fin
   so late in the night
   so late in the century
    in the 20th Century

.

FROM

FOR THE LOVE OF A COAT

(1978)

SELAVIE

Why is it so hard to start exactly where I'm at?
Not yesterday in the refuse or tomorrow in Italy
but from the puff of smoke curling over the blue
of my manly Smith Corona 220, a smoke signal
to my mother for her to send new clippings about cancer
from Reader's Digest, The Washington Post and the
National Geographic.   Everywhere someone is defending
a piece of the picturesque.   Maybe there isn't
anything to start with but that's absurd since every second
the dough rises and the bell is about to ring.
A mad black dog will walk through the door.
A howling will begin in the red telephone.
The posters will fall from the wall.   The working class
might be rising. Night might fall. Wind may blow. Rain may
drench us to the bone and cold may eat our noses.
And yet, the American way is to keep working.
Sombitches these Americans, father dies, brother drowns,
wife runs away but the logs must go down the river.
The trucks are waiting and the goods must move.

STOCK REPORT

Nobody speaks of it but destiny is currency today
and the new market is the human psyche
vaster than continents much grander than geography.
Today's capitalists look within.
From the quirks of your free flights hang the products of
          tomorrow!
As for me, Sir, I don't have any feelings.   I just have gods.

Right now I am the favorite of Depression, a mean and petty
    god with dirty fingers.
Yesterday I happened to tangle with Love, by the river.
When the people have no more feelings
the gods turn to each other for company and stagger the world
with imaginative pageants, slaughters, miracles and ruins.
Tomorrow's man will be a voyeur wishing for night
under the faucet of stars too bright for sleep.
Get hold if you can of a little room all black buried in a
velvet bale under the ground without windows
and return the valve from where it was removed.
We must be absolutely without importance
until we regain our advantages.
Then one day we will stage a magnificent revolt.

A GOOD THING WHEN I SEE ONE

Good thing I'm in a dark room eating rocks.
I could be in the light stroking the lizard on my arm.
If it takes
the government, the police, the publishers, the spiders
and whoever else is after me—and if they aren't
why I talk is beyond me—for a decent sacrifice
I will certainly rip their guts with my own Swiss army knife.
Now those are old offerings and perhaps
only my heart will do
or my brain or my lungs or my feet or my eyes
maybe I should be a nazi crushing the fingers of my piano hand!
It takes a lot.   It takes a lot of nerve.   It takes me by surprise.
It takes all it can get.   It takes the getting.   It takes
the getting up.   It takes my wallet, my watch and my keys.
It takes friends.   It takes friends by the throat.   It takes
the cultivation of reality.   It takes reality.   It gives
reality.   It takes reality.   It gives reality.

À FRANCIS PONGE

Unlike virtue
style doesn't require any examples.   Examples can use
the extra time to acquire style.   They could mount
a campaign against being called Examples.   They could
be Events.   We don't want to be examples.   We just want
to happen.   Where would the police be without examples?
Where the professor?   Where the state?   Where the censor?

ODE TO CURIOSITY

It isn't just spying that turns me on.
It's also the spyglass for having
so much light as to have no memory
though it retains the feeling.
Truly, there is no perfect opaqueness in nature.
Someone is looking through me at you just as
through you
someone is staring at me.
Ah, to be a beautiful narcissist wrapped
like Christmas paper around
a gentle voyeur!
This is what I want, Seigneur!
And then to glide out of focus.

Drowning Another Peasant Inquisition

Jealousy runs only skin deep.
Underneath lies the joy of not possessing.
Thus spoke the sage caressing
his one and only claim to love

as all were seated, thinking

Between friends silence is your best bet,
he continued.
O oneness of bodies firmly planted breasts
and proudly set cocks

as on the streets, the rest
are pulled along by long streaks of bad luck

of which we know the reason.
The many windows framed in yellow light
are pulled together making
mind structures, more mind chains
around the masses falling through the season.

One day to see
One day you will be free

That day you come and see me
That day you see me, hear

"MAN" AND "WOMAN," these are horrid words, they annoy me. They chase me through the world these two, hunting my spirit with a damp blanket of grim assumptions. "MAN" is a load of perilous experience hardening inside something called "MATURITY" like a boiled hotdog into an inflating blanket of dough or a limp air mattress into which a frantic tourist blows his lungs as the ship burns, and "WOMAN" is somebody who will look through every one of my gestures with a gaze loaded with sandpaper and after making me entirely transparent puts her boot through the glass. I much prefer boys and girls.   I much prefer girls and boys.   I much prefer innocence. I much prefer blind love and joy.

Sunday Sermon

All sound is religion.
Language is merely a choir boy in this religion.
Sometimes a bishop wind rattles the windows.
Still, I must speak the most intelligent language available
while I have this typewriter knowing full well that tomorrow
I might be able to welcome a color Xerox machine into my studio
and with it there will be a revolution in my life.
And this revolution will wipe out the need for words.
I will say nothing for a few years to prepare for a new
revolution. Revolution. The word is like a revolver on a
sunlit window sill. It is one of the few words that sets
my heart on fire. Girl also sets my heart on fire.
Girl & Revolution. Revolution & Girl.
I am twelve years old and I intend to stay that way.

It takes joy to listen and it is inspiring being listened to. People who half-listen are half-inspiring. But I will go half and half with you if we fuck too.   Fucking makes up in intensity the half that isn't listening.   And it makes up the unlistened half too.   In fact, we will fuck in the cemetery where no one is listening and no one is listened to.   Listen to me.   I will listen to you.

Ode to Laryngitis

With the collapse of the vocal chords and through
the graces of laryngitis, a new perception of reality
knocked me off my divan and twisting my arms,
delivered me dripping at the gates of heaven.
Where it entered my eyes, my brain, my hands
and left me speechless with occult new beauty.
The cracked voice in this throat is mine
and the oddly shaped vowels coming out of it are
the remains of the writing voice talking about
the speaking voice, the remains also of a mellifluous
bowing to bourgeois use of speech which English,
in its ever expanding luminous wisdom, has set
right on the surface for easier notice and faster disposal.
Remains, remains, and then: a pure vowel.   And another.

Fascination

People pass under my windows deeply absorbed in garter belts
but they have not come for me.   I tower here above their red
lit brains, whipped by the sandpaper wind that blows the skin
off lovers' wrists, not by a piece of the action.   A leaflet
too blows by.   A long read, a short story.

One day there is a party for the whole galaxy
and the ghost weeping for his lips remembers his lines.
The horse looks at himself in the water and sees a black harmonica.
The melancholy robot dances in the black box.
One day the profound evil is deprived of its music
and stripped both of its profundity and its intense satisfaction.

With a great heave the tree of my life topples
to give way to shiny rails.
I am exhaled, squeezed tight, pressed on and loved.

EPITAPH

He was a young guy with surrealist connections.
this tombstone does not lie
it merely stands imbedded in the sweet dark stew
waiting for the connoisseur

LOVE THINGS

"I would suppress my gastric
functions like the moon to coolly
appraise the fruits," said she

and set me thinking that whatever follows
results in logic and logic is
for the use of money

and this place, with her in it, did not
follow at all, no it did not
follow

but love did.

Great fucking followed and the poems,
made un-natural by sophistication,
were read with great innocence

and in this way
became natural again.

It wasn't in what she said but in what seemed
to lie like a panther behind
her clothes,

a great authority, a thousand
small commands soldered together
by a brilliant generalisation:

CUT OFF THAT HEAD!

The esoteric truth is that when love
is the key
it does not much matter
what or whom one loves

because, instead of her, it could have been a thing
making me feel this way.
Perhaps it was.

A voodoo thing, a visual conglomerate.

All this was clear because
unloved things are massive
blocks to vision

so that between you and god stand
the vast masses of unloved
things

bumping into each other in misprint,
mishearing, mistranslation and mistakes.

Since I cannot love all things
and love is knocking my perceptions
off their feet, I will

ignore what I don't love.

Tomorrow, I will ignore you much as
I love you now

because I want to bring myself
to love all things
to find, inside all things,
their claim to me, the place where
their sexuality is hidden.

For all things have
a claim to my love.

Curtains, curtains, Iron Curtain,
I am tearing you up.

The mind, a yellow boomerang, heads
for the piled bananas

filling the two purple hoolahoops
under my eyes.

I want to love
without qualification
everything I do

even if much of what I do
has no love in it and this,

to my mind, means
that it is meant for someone else
to find the love in it.

Even if I don't
put it in there
something else does

so that all creation
is objectively valid, and the magnetic

positioning of one's self
does not destroy the flow.

If you resemble, imitate or parody me
I will not love you.

Likeness, the crucial communication.
Compassion, the messenger of it.

I formulated this after the fact
of you, and it was only
the fact of you that mattered.

The directness of you because only
the most direct
has any claim to me

and veiled things are meant
for someone else:
I am no rapist!

but I do
love love and that is
where it stands

AT HOME

Small crimes, like pepper, make things
taste better.
Only very exotic people can commit large crimes
and not burn their mouths.
Spices, like crimes, are based
on various transgressions of the laws,
natural or social, so that
the feast, when it begins,
will cure the cells of definition.
Oh, what dishes won't we have,
says mother seeing
the world, that sudden
bite of food, that sudden shutting of a thousand
mouths on a thousand nipples.
Oh we shall have it all and then
we shall sleep.

THE LOVE OF A COAT

It has been uppermost in my mind to write about my clothes which
are not much as clothes go but do their job in a suitable manner. I
have two shirts one red one purple which I never wear and a great
many T-shirts which look much better on my wife with her nipples
rippling the cloth through the cloth I should say. The same is true
about my two pair of bluejeans which have been ageing separately
but gracefully around both of our asses. The coat which loves me the
most is a French paratrooper's army jacket and I could tell of this love
by the way in which it still looks good after its pockets are filled with
various stolen books, steaks and loose change. The other coats love
me less, but no matter, I brave the rain & wind in them. In addition to

these vestments there are the silk and velvet things all embroidered
with gold & silver which sit on the bottom of secret closets waiting
for a great day. This day is getting closer and closer and I can tell
by the desperation in the love of my daily getup that the day to
give up my familiar self is looking through the windows already.

Don't Wait for Me

People wait for their mail, dogs wait for their can,
farmers wait for rain, everybody waits for death,
everybody but me.   I'm not waiting for nuttin.
I would imagine I would sit down to commit suicide.
It takes a lot of nerve to commit suicide standing up.
But being in a doghouse while childhood
sprinkles sand on my ass is better than either position.
The fact is, other people are waiting for me
to tell them this,
they are waiting to see me lay my white wrist on the VegeoMatic.
I disappoint them.
I'm a mean Motherfucker.

The Goldrush

I paint my nails gold.
My face I also paint gold.
My body is gold already.
These gold shoes are from Provence.
Cock, solid gold.

My voice, a gold frog leaping on a gold rug.
My eyes only notice gold while I
naturally only touch gold.
In order to afford all this I work
in a pitch dark basement with a fellow I have
never seen.
Things, you know, have a golden glow.

MUFFLED BY A BELT ACROSS THE MOUTH

Words are really tiny.
The mouth is much bigger.   It can take
two hundred million words to close a mouth.
Even then someone would
hang a sign on it which says   OPEN
like the diner across the street which is
always closed.
Maybe we die with a mouth full of words.
Maybe this is why the dead speak
mainly to unassuming folks who never
talk unless asked.
Things being as they are, I do not trust the grave.
Be quiet, love

Against Meaning

Everything I do is against meaning.
This is partly deliberate, mostly spontaneous.
Wherever I am I think I'm somewhere else.
This is partly to confuse the police, mostly to
avoid myself es-
pecially when I have to confirm
the obvious which always
sits on a little table and draws a lot
of attention to itself.
So much so that no one sees the chairs
and the girl sitting on one of them.
With the obvious one is always at the movies.
The other obvious which the loud obvious
conceals
is not obvious enough to merit a
surrender of the will.
But through a little hole in the boring report
God watches us faking it.

The Threat

I am not looking for your jugular.
Only for your eyes.

This isn't exactly accurate.
I want both.   And if you ask, as you should
if you like yourself, why do I go for such
ferocious treats, I must
admit

that there is something unexploded in my gut.

And it wants you because there is
an unexploded something in yours too.

A music box we swallowed when we were children?
The growing up?   Which is
learning to handle terror?
Was there something in the food or is
the government responsible for it?

It's nothing I can stick my knife into and say:
"For sure it's this!"

And yet I want it out more than I want these words

FROM
NECROCORRIDA
(1980)

À FACE

I have been altered like a suit
to accommodate a much larger man.
Dedication & appalling motives support this enlargement
like crossbeams in a simple church in Transylvania.
I have gone against nature
and now I have fur.
I am the most ruthlessly hunted
but the most ecologically abundant animal.
My name is victory over mother and father.

NEAR SONNET

I carry in my wallet the replica, cast in shell,
of Maria's clitoris.
Others have pictures in their wallets.
Adieu, flat surfaces. From now on I will carry sculptures.
When shipwrecked on the reefs of love
you find yourself hallucinating the light-house signal
coming from the tip of your cock, take thee off thine feet
and search the rocks for a totemic shape

Love Poem (for Alice)

Some things exclude each other ferociously but
in a Loving Manner! I cannot imagine
you anything but beautiful because to do
otherwise is to witness
the Collapse of Imagination like the collapse
of the L train in Chicago which has to be seen
to be Imagined.
A Thought Reader with Moral Hangups
is Inconceivable! Who is also a reader
of cardiovascular changes like a gold scarab
in an old library.
Imagination is so that I can sleep like a reptile
on a warm egg surrounded by your presence
So that you can Come Back when I want you to

The West Is the Best and the Future Is Near

A long gold nail from the Goldrush
nails shut the box inside of which
California squirms with unbearable visions
of the Future
I am looking for my face in the Future like a straw
ploughing the cocktail for another cherry
Is Anybody There? Am I there in my
moonbeam jacket crossing the street against the light
to take another look at you? And the light yet
trails the unweary detective into the trains
where the Sea swells

Perhaps my face is the horizon in the crack
between the worlds like the clouds
in Alice's pictures of sunsets

ODE TO MEXICO

It is a Pleasure being Alive in the Arms of Form
dreaming of Mexico! Going to Mexico!
The need I have for you, Mexico,
makes you real though my hair is long and the Thalidomide
Bobsey Twins patrol the borders
with shiny scissors protruding from the butt of their rifles
as if to say "Hairstyles are the Angles
of the Domestication of Power!" which is what
they mean not what they say
unaware that the angels are watching.
Meanwhile the Great Siesta goes on!
A year from now perhaps I will be in Italy
looking at the frescoes but remembering Mexico
like the face of a moviestar in which unexpressed feelings
lie under the lid of a stoned smile
as Oaxaca boils under the jungle sun without
a thought! As my hair keeps growing & shifting
my position until I lose from view the small
fires burning in the dimming summer hours!

Love Simmers the Stew of the Dead
(to the amateur photographers on Market Street)

It is me you photograph
when I pass tall and dark but not unfriendly
pressed on by urban need like a daffodil
on the chest of a dead Austrian Sergeant
on my way to one bus or another
through the movies of amphibious old ladies
blowing up the bingo cafeterias
It is me you would like to invite to dinner
Content to squeeze me into mouldy images instead
And it is you I would like to photograph
because Spring is here and soon
I will be in far away lands

Irony as Nursery

"The inspired evil and the uninspired good,
said the table set for two,
are dining inside you"   Flying creatures
filled with transcendental irony like creme
de menthe flit by.   I am again, naturally
talking to myself in the manner
of a small saloon. The body is a small saloon
doing all the talking to the creature in my head
which is a spider.   While the heart
continues to be a miracle and the scenario
of the face rages publicly.   And then to think,
miserably, over a cup of coffee, how the map
is all dots of jailed men hanging
from bare electric bulbs in underground prisons

swaying between light as we see it
and the wall of light in the dark.
And when thought out all the way and seen
from all the angles, the joy of its presence, the joy of
its constancy

BALLAD OF THE TYPIST

Wet skeletons play wet harmonicas in the electric
typewriter, to drive the typist mad who would rather be out,
in fine weather, not in with his Personality.
But he remembers all the beds in his life,
some made neatly, some unmade, some made of earth,
some made of blood, some made of books, and all
the bodies floating over them:
bits of himself stick out of everyone like broken arrows.
It appears now that the whole race is practicing karate
to eliminate the weather and keep him in:
Italians walk slapping each others' backs toward the Future,
Rumanians with balled fists punch holes through the Scarecrow.
Hungarians pinch the half moons of each others' asses and Giggle,
at the end of piers French men and women kiss incessantly in the Rain,
under tanks oily Russians hug each other attempting to Turn Over,
in neon lit rooms Americans shake with one hand in their Pockets.
The Chinese would rather bow.
Armies go, leaving their exhibitionists behind.
God gives you tongue, the devil gives you hands,
the eyes are of an even stranger make.
The typing finger alone, ponders the unmade.

Model Work

I model myself after someone I made up at ten walking
the mazes of my medieval city's streets, a being
so light, so bright, so fast, so generous and so complete
he almost had no body, only a black hat. Furthermore
he appeared only in the rain. To this day
he cannot be mauled because he is both outside & in.
When I think of him I feel the sorrow of my later models.
The word was a worthy model once when I had a typewriter.
Modelling is a warm march through grace without recourse.
Only the loveliest and strongest models run the course.
There is a rush to model and new models are proposed.
But there isn't a country where there are no models.
There is no rock that will not model, or sand or fruit.

The shadow in my blood will model for a fee.
And yet a lake of absent possibilities has risen
to the chin of the folk, and the waters keep rising
for what could be a model drowning.
I conversed with the drownees. What they said
turned my love for myself into syllables.
Will I be a model for my son or only endless buzzing?

The Masses Are Constantly on the Telephone

I have one more question but I will not ask it because Charles
Manson is a testimony to the power of collage as an art form. Not all
art forms, of course, can boast of a perfect literalist of Charlie's
stature but since there are no new forms one hopes they will some-
day. Fucking isn't a new form yet it's always a pleasure and occa-

sionally there is a Cassanova or a Marie-Antoinette to place an exclamation mark after the obvious! The beautiful actors brush their teeth singing the Dictionary while I sit in the waiting room taking Telephone Calls from the Masses. It *is* a dirty business, doctor, but we do not rely on gravity as much as you would like us to think.

REMEMBRANCE OF MY FORGOTTEN SKINNINESS

I was a man so skinny light travelled with a
horrendous thump upward through my only vein
which the folks, naturally alert, would point
out to each other at night as I stalked
the mains of natural gas.
Often mistaken for a street lamp I would suffer
the gold urine of the ruined bums.
All this time I was nothing. I had no purpose.
A hack doctor polishing with spit a scalpel.
A wall in a church where they've buried a tractor.
I was a man so skinny I stuck to paper
and screamed at the letters.
The lettuce of desire dragged me down.
The weight of the podium could be measured in hogs.
In the bags themselves I wouldn't fit.
But when I came to America the situation changed.
Today I am a solid bank of meat.
I have just eaten critter.

A STILL

I do not move my hands any longer, I do not
shift my legs, my eyes look straight ahead, I confine
my delirium to my blood, I have,
like Monsieur Teste, killed my puppet
with the calm in my mind.
I have struck a blow into the center where
the racial and the personal puppet
balanced each other like clowns on a tightrope which is
what happens when a continent has just been discovered
and the discoverers are having the time of their lives
stretching their language to fit the chill.
Oh the spectacle of thousands of naked owners
in private fields of blood
killing their puppets with their bare legs
like diseased chickens
and then owning nothing, finally.
This is a Discovery which lies in the Future.
Walt Whitman, who reclines in the Future
is readying the house for the party

PAPER ON HUMOR

Everything sounds funny in a funny magazine.
For years now I have published my poems in funny magazines
so that nobody would notice
how sad they were.
Sad anthologists, however, took my poems out of context
and put them in the sad anthologies and there
they started to shine with tears because
they were the saddest poems in there.

With a liking for funnies
and a following of sadness followers
I arrive in Brazil to get my prize.
The prize consists of the cross, the guillotine
and the hot pepper.
I am collected. Nothing matters to me.